westermann

Bumblebee

Textbook 4
Baden-Württemberg

Herausgegeben von
Gisela Ehlers

Erarbeitet von
Gisela Ehlers und Michaela Schönau

Auf der Grundlage der Ausgaben
Bumblebee Textbook 4 Bayern (2015),
Bumblebee Textbook 4 (2013) und
Bumblebee Textbook 4 (2017) von
Gisela Ehlers, Grit Kahstein,
Christina Meindl, Ursula Michailow-Drews,
Anna Van Montagu, Matthias Muth,
Michaela Schönau, Hannelore Tait
und Anne Zeich-Pelsis

Muttersprachliche Beratung
Elspeth Corrie

Illustriert von
Juliane Assies, Jutta Garbert,
Angela Glökler, Heike Heimrich,
Gabie Hilgert, Elisabeth Holzhausen,
Karoline Kehr, Oda Ruthe,
Friederike Schumann und
Ulrike Vetter

Contents

▸ Ich kann verstehen, was die Kinder über sich sagen.

Hello

1 Listen and point.

2 Listen again and talk about the children.

3 Talk about yourself.

Back at school

1 What can you name in the picture?

2 Listen and point.

3 Practise the questions.

Fragen im Klassenzimmer.
Diff ▼ KV 8
Wdh: Can you / Can I ... ?

- FC/WC 1–13
- CD 2/3, KV 6–8
- WB S. 4

▸ Ich kann Fragen im Unterricht stellen.

What school things can you name?
Can you say the numbers?
Can you name the colours?

Who can you see?
Can you read the date?

▸ Ich kann etwas über Schulen in England erzählen.

Raptime

It's English now,
speak, speak, speak!

Then it's maths,
count, count, count!

It's German now,
read, read, read!

Now it's art,
draw, draw, draw!

Music next,
sing, sing, sing!

Golden time,
fun, fun, fun.

1 Listen and read along. 

2 Do the rap. 

Hi Leute,
die Schule hat wieder angefangen und wir haben unseren neuen Stundenplan bekommen.
Da gibt es zum Beispiel das Fach *ICT*. Das steht für *Information and Communication Technology*. Hier lernen wir, am Computer zu arbeiten. Das macht Spaß. Das Fach *science* ist auch sehr interessant. Wir lernen eine Menge über Pflanzen und Tiere und machen Experimente. Wenn wir *golden time* haben, können wir uns aussuchen, was wir am liebsten machen möchten. Ich hole mir dann gern Bücher aus unserer Bücherei *(library)*. In *PE (Physical Education)* spielen wir oft Teamspiele. In der Pause sind wir auf dem *school playground*, dem Schulhof. Wir spielen gern Himmel und Hölle *(hopscotch)* oder Fangspiele wie *What's the time, Mr Wolf?*
Love Lisa

3 Sprecht über Lisas Brief.

4 Wisst ihr noch mehr über englische Schulen?

Landeskundliche Informationen über Schulen in Großbritannien erhalten.
Den *School rap* (CD 4/5) singen.

- FC 15, 16, 18, 19, 21, 24
- CD 4/5

▸ Ich kann über meinen Stundenplan sprechen.

School subjects

1 music

2 PE

3 art

4 golden time

5 assembly

6 English

7 maths

8 German

9 ICT

10 science

11 crafts

		9.15 – 10.15		10.15 – 11.30	11.30 – 12.30		1.30 – 2.30	2.30 – 3.30
Monday	assembly	maths	break	English	PE	school dinner	science	crafts
Tuesday		maths		English	German		science	PE
Wednesday		maths		English	music		project	
Thursday		maths		English	art		ICT	PE
Friday		maths		English	ICT		German	golden time

On Mondays I have maths, English, PE, science and crafts.

1 Listen and point.

2 Talk to a partner.

3 Write your timetable in English.

Die Unterrichtsfächer benennen können.
Einen Stundenplan vorstellen.

• FC/WC 14–24
• CD 6/7, KV 9
• WB S. 5

▸ Ich kann sagen, warum ich ein Fach mag oder nicht.

Let's talk: What I like about school

I like …
I don't like …

I like …	music	because	speaking.
	maths	I like …	drawing.
	German		reading.
	English		singing.
I don't like …	PE		learning about nature.
	art	because	counting.
	crafts	I don't like …	building things.
	science		moving around.

1 Listen and read along.

2 Practise the dialogue.

3 Make a list: I like … / I don't like …

Begründen, warum man ein Fach mag oder nicht.
Diff ▲ KV 11, Diff ▼ KV 12–14
Wdh: I like / don't like

• FC/WC 14–24
• CD 8
• KV 11–14, 16

▸ Ich kann eine Geschichte nachspielen.

School of the future

1 Listen and point.

2 Listen again and read along.

3 What did you understand?

4 Do a role-play.

Eine Geschichte verstehen und nachspielen.
Diff ▼ L liest die Geschichte selbst.
Diff ▲ Die Geschichte mit KV 17/93 selbst erzählen.

- SC 1–6
- CD 9, KV 17/93
- How to do a role-play (S. 59)

Dress for the weather

1 Listen and point.

2 Talk about the picture.

Über Wetterlagen und Kleidung sprechen.
Diff ▲ KV 21, Diff ▼ KV 20
Wdh: Seasons

- FC/WC 25–45
- CD 12/13
- KV 18–22

▶ Ich kann Wetterlagen, Jahreszeiten und Kleidungsstücke benennen.

What are the children doing?
How many boots / ... can you see?
What can you see / read on the board?

Can you name the seasons?
What is your favourite season?

Football jerseys

Hallo Leute,

gestern habe ich mit meinem Daddy Fußball geschaut. Das war ganz schön spannend! Manchester United hat gegen den Celtic Football Club gespielt. Mein Daddy hat mir erklärt, dass die Trikots der Vereine traditionelle Farben oder Abzeichen haben. Bei Manchester United ist das Trikot rot mit Streifen an den Seiten. Ben, der ein großer ManU Fan ist, hat mir erzählt, dass die Streifen an Eisenbahnschienen erinnern sollen. Früher haben nämlich viele Menschen in Manchester bei der Eisenbahn gearbeitet und die meisten Spieler waren Eisenbahnarbeiter.
Das finde ich ganz schön interessant. Habe mir gleich mal im Internet angesehen, warum das Trikot der Celtic-FC-Spieler grünweiß-gestreift ist. Dort habe ich das gefunden: Die Vereinsfarben Grün und Weiß sind auf die Landesflagge von Irland zurückzuführen, da die Spieler von Celtic früher größtenteils irischer Herkunft waren.
Wie ist denn das in Deutschland?
Seid ihr Fans eines Fußballklubs? Haben die auch traditionelle Farben?

Liebe Grüße und bis bald
Lisa

1 Lest Lisas E-Mail.

2 Was wisst ihr noch über Vereinstrikots?

▸ Ich kann beschreiben, welche Kleidung Leute tragen.

Let's talk: Find someone who is wearing ...

1 Listen and point.

2 Play the guessing game.

Ray and his raincoat

1 Listen to the song.

2 Sing along. Do a role-play.

Einen Song verstehen.
Ray and his raincoat (CD 15/16) singen.

- CD 15/16
- KV 27

The lost wallet

1 Listen and read along.

2 Do a role-play.

My day

1 Listen and point.

2 Talk about Emma's day.

3 Make a poster and present it.

Den eigenen Tagesablauf vorstellen.
Diff ▲ KV 34, Diff ▼ KV 35/36
Wdh: Hobbies, time

- FC/WC 46–57
- CD 19/20, KV 31–36, WB S. 13/14
- How to do a presentation (S. 58)

▸ Ich kann über meinen Tagesablauf berichten.

Who is giving a presentation?
Who is standing next to the board?
Do you know other daily routines?

What can you see on the poster?
What do you do in the morning / in the afternoon / in the evening?

Time in Great Britain: a.m. and p.m.

Hey ihr in Deutschland,
ihr glaubt nicht, was mir gestern passiert ist. Das war so peinlich. Ben hatte mich zum Geburtstag eingeladen. In der Einladung stand *Come to my birthday party at 6:30 p.m.*
Als ich bei Ben ankam, öffnete er erst nach dem zweiten Klingeln. Er war erstaunt mich zu sehen. Als ich ihm erklärte, dass auf seiner Einladung doch 6:30 stand, musste er plötzlich so lachen. Er erklärte mir, dass bei englischen Uhrzeiten immer ein *a.m.* oder *p.m.* nach den Ziffern stehen würde: *A.m.* bezeichnet die Stunden von Mitternacht bis Mittag (also den Vormittag) und *p.m.* die Stunden von Mittag bis Mitternacht (also den Nachmittag). Ben hat mir sogar noch eine Eselsbrücke erklärt: *a.m. – at morning* (am Morgen), *p.m. – past morning* (nach dem Morgen). Ursprünglich kommen diese Bezeichnungen aus dem Lateinischen: *ante meridiem (a.m.)* und *post meridiem (p.m.)*.
Ich bin dann nochmal nach Hause gefahren und abends wieder hin.
Die anderen haben ganz schön gelacht, als sie von meinem Missgeschick erfahren haben.

Bis bald,
Lisa

1 Lest Lisas Brief.

2 Wie viele verschiedene Arten die Uhrzeit anzugeben kennt ihr?

Uhrzeitangaben mit *a.m.* und *p.m.* kennenlernen.
Wdh: Numbers

▸ Ich kann verstehen, wann sich Emma verabredet.

Emma's diary

1 Listen and point to the days.

2 Listen again. When will Emma, Ben and Ravi meet?

3 Talk about your week.

Lots of hobbies

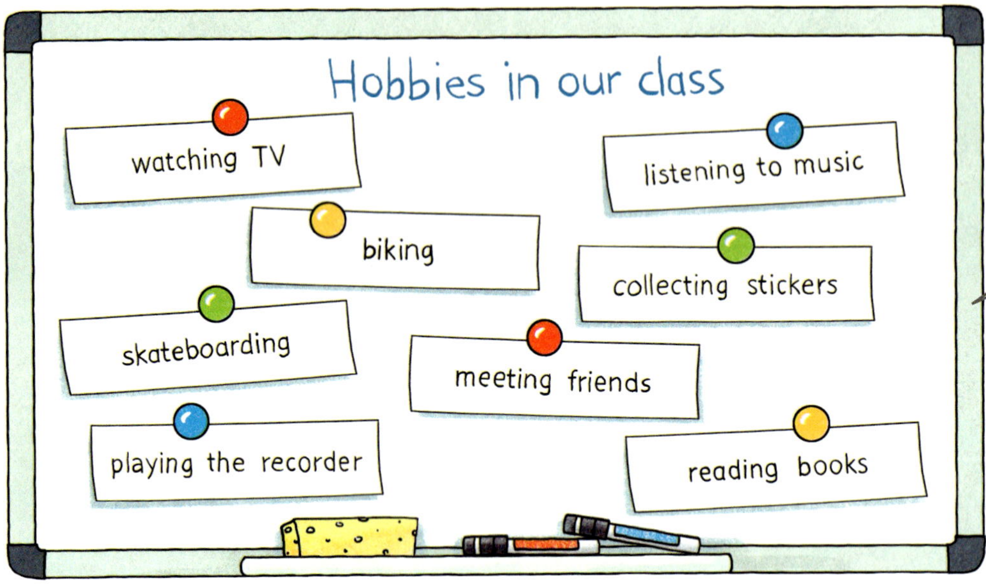

I like ...

 Lisa	 Linda	 Paul	 Ben
 Emma	 Simon	 Ravi	 Elly

Ravi likes biking. True or false?

False. Ravi likes collecting football stickers.

1 Read the hobbies.

2 Talk about the children's hobbies.

Hobbys von Freunden vorstellen.
Diff ▲ KV 39
Wdh: Hobbies

• FC/WC 58–65
• KV 39
• WB S. 15

▸ Ich kann mich mit anderen verabreden.

Let's talk: When can we meet?

1 Ask a question.

2 Spin the bottle.

3 Take a Bingo card. Say the sentence.

1 Listen to the children.

2 Practise the dialogue.

3 Play the game.

Tipp

In the morning
In the afternoon
In the evening

At home

1 Listen, read and speak along.

2 Talk about the picture.

Über die Einrichtung eines Zimmers sprechen.
Diff ▲ KV 44, Diff ▼ KV 43

- FC/WC 66–82
- CD 26/27, KV 41–44
- WB S. 16

▸ Ich kann Räume und Möbel benennen.

What can you see on the poster?
Who can you see in the picture?
What are the children doing?

Where do you live? In a flat or a house?
How many rooms have you got?
What is in the children's bedroom?

▸ Ich kann etwas über Häuser in Großbritannien sagen.

Homes in Great Britain

Hallo ihr in Deutschland,
ich war neulich bei Ben zu Besuch. Weil der Akku von meinem Handy leer war, wollte ich es aufladen. Dabei habe ich mal wieder gemerkt, dass mein Stecker gar nicht passt. Ich glaube, das hab ich euch noch gar nicht erzählt. Seitdem wir nach England gezogen sind, brauchen wir für unsere elektronischen Geräte einen Adapter. Das liegt daran, dass Steckdosen *(sockets)* und Stecker *(plugs)* in England anders aussehen als in Deutschland.
Eine weitere Besonderheit in England ist, dass fast jedes Haus mehrere Schornsteine *(chimneys)* auf dem Dach hat. Denn in jedem Wohnzimmer gibt es einen Kamin mit einem elektrischen Feuer, den *fireplace*. Außerdem gibt's in englischen Häusern keine *cellars*, also Keller. Das finde ich super, ich hab nämlich tierisch Angst vor Spinnen!

Viele Grüße von Lisa

1 Lest Lisas E-Mail.

2 Vergleicht englische Häuser mit Häusern und Wohnungen, die ihr kennt.

Etwas über Häuser in Großbritannien erfahren.

▸ Ich kann andere nach ihrem Traumzuhause fragen.

Let's talk: My dream home

Which rooms would you like to have in your dream home?

I'd like to have a big kitchen and five bedrooms.

What would you like to have, a garden or a balcony?

A garden with a big swimming pool.

What would you like to have in your bedroom?

In my bedroom I'd like to have two wardrobes, a bed and lots of bookshelves.

I'd like =
I would like

1 Listen and read along.

2 Practise the dialogue.

▸ Ich kann eine Wegbeschreibung verstehen.

Can you tell me the way?

You are here

turn left

go straight ahead

turn right

Excuse me, can you tell me the way to Baker Street?

Thank you very much.

Go straight ahead. Then turn right into Queen's Road.

Go straight ahead and turn left into Baker Street.

1 Look at the map. What can you see?

2 Listen and find the way on the map.

Eine Wegbeschreibung verstehen.
Diff ▲ Eine Wegbeschreibung geben, KV 49
Diff ▼ KV 48

• FC/WC 83–85
• CD 29, KV 48/49
• WB S. 19

Tidy up your room

1 Listen and point.

2 Describe the 2 pictures.

3 Write about the pictures.

4 Think of an ending.

At the zoo

1 Listen and point.

2 Which animals would you like to see?

3 Plan your day at the zoo.

Zootiere benennen und beschreiben. Ein Plakat lesen.
Diff ▲ KV 55, Diff ▼ KV 56
Wdh: Time, pets

• FC/WC 93–115
• CD 37/38, KV 52–56

▸ Ich kann Zootiere benennen.

Which animals can you see?
When is the feeding time for ...?
Do you know any zoos?

Which animals do you remember?
What else can you see in the picture?

▸ Ich kann Texte über Tiere auf Deutsch wiedergeben.

Animals around the world

Panda bears live in bamboo forests in the mountains of China.
Pandas eat bamboo leaves.
They can live up to 30 years.
They are endangered.

There are about 60 million kangaroos in Australia.
They can jump high and far.
They have a pouch to carry their babies.
They eat plants.
They can live up to 25 years.

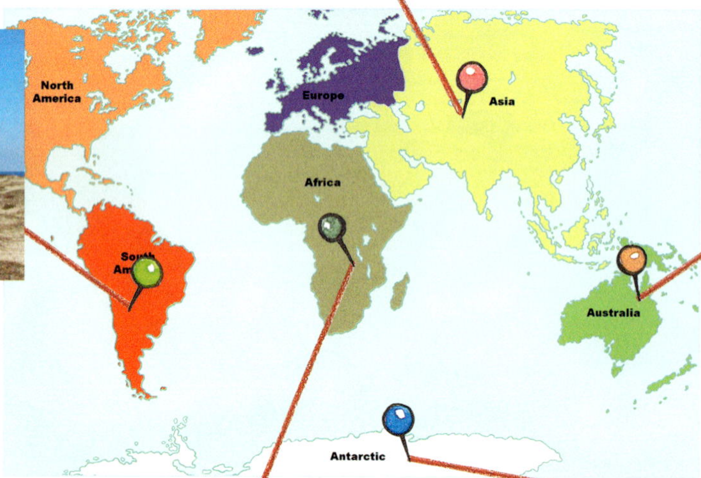

Llamas live in the mountains of South America.
Llamas eat plants.
When they feel attacked, they bite, kick or spit.
People drink their milk and use their wool.

Penguins live in Antarctica.
They are birds with two flippers and two feet.
They lay eggs. Penguins can't fly but they can dive up to 900 metres.
They eat fish.

Lions are big cats that live in the grassland and savannah of Africa.
The male lion has a mane.
Lions live and hunt in families.
Lions eat meat. They can roar loudly.
They can live up to 14 years.

1 Listen and point.

2 Talk about the animals.

Mediation: Die Texte auf Deutsch besprechen.

• FC/WC 102, 105, 110, 116, 117
• CD 39, KV 57

▸ Ich kann etwas über den Londoner Zoo erzählen.

The lion sleeps tonight

Text/Musik: L. Creatore, S. Linda, H. Peretti, G. Weiss

Hallo ihr in Deutschland!
Den Londoner Zoo gibt es seit 1828. Er ist riesig! Man kann dort über 700 verschiedene Tierarten sehen. Ein Tag reicht dafür gar nicht aus. Am besten gefallen mir die Tierfütterungen, weil die Tierpfleger *(zookeeper)* dabei Interessantes über die Tiere erzählen und unsere Fragen beantworten. Es gibt da ein tolles Angebot, bei dem man einen Tag lang als Hilfstierpfleger oder -pflegerin *(keeper for a day)* im Zoo mitarbeiten darf. Ben und ich wollten uns gleich für einen der Ferientage anmelden, aber man muss mindestens 16 Jahre alt sein. Schade!

Eure Lisa

1 Listen and sing the song.

2 Sprecht über Lisas Brief.

Informationen über den Londoner Zoo erhalten.
The lion sleeps tonight (CD 40/41) singen.

• CD 40/41
• WB S. 22

Chimpanzees: Endangered animals

Chimpanzees are big apes that live in the forests of Central Africa.
Chimpanzees are not monkeys because they do not have a tail.
They are endangered because people destroy their world.
There are rangers who protect their areas in the forests.
Their natural enemies are leopards and snakes.
Chimpanzees are shy animals. They are noisy and intelligent.
They live in big groups of 30 to 80 animals.
The strongest chimpanzee is the boss of the group.
He protects the mothers and babies.
Chimpanzees sleep in tree nests.
They eat fruit, nuts and flowers as well as insects and meat.

Height:	1 – 1.7 metres
Weight:	35 – 70 kilograms
Food:	Fruits, plants, some meat
Life span:	Up to 40 years
Enemies:	Leopards, snakes, people

1 Wo leben die Schimpansen?
2 Wodurch sind sie gefährdet?
3 Welche Eigenschaften haben sie?
4 Wovon ernähren sie sich?

1 What is the text about?

2 Listen and read along.

3 Beantwortet die Fragen auf Deutsch.

Let's talk: New at the zoo

Penguins	**Chimpanzees**	**Parrots**	**Camels**
Habitat: Antarctic	Habitat: Jungle	Habitat: Rainforest	Habitat: Desert
Food: Fish	Food: Bananas	Food: Fruit	Food: Fruit/grass
Life span: 12 years	Life span: 40 years	Life span: 50 years	Life span: 40 years

Where do chimpanzees live?

Chimpanzees live in the jungle.

What do chimpanzees eat?

They eat bananas.

How old can chimpanzees get?

They can get to 40 years old.

Can they climb?

Yes, they can.

1 Listen to the keeper's talk and read along.

2 Talk about the other animals.

3 Do a role-play.

Tipp

Where, where, where, wo kommst du her?

Fakten über Tiere erfragen und weitergeben.
Diff ▲ 60, Diff ▼ 61
Den *Zookeeper rap* (KV 66, CD 47/48) singen.

• CD 43, (47/48)
• WB S. 21
• KV 60/61/66

A trip to London

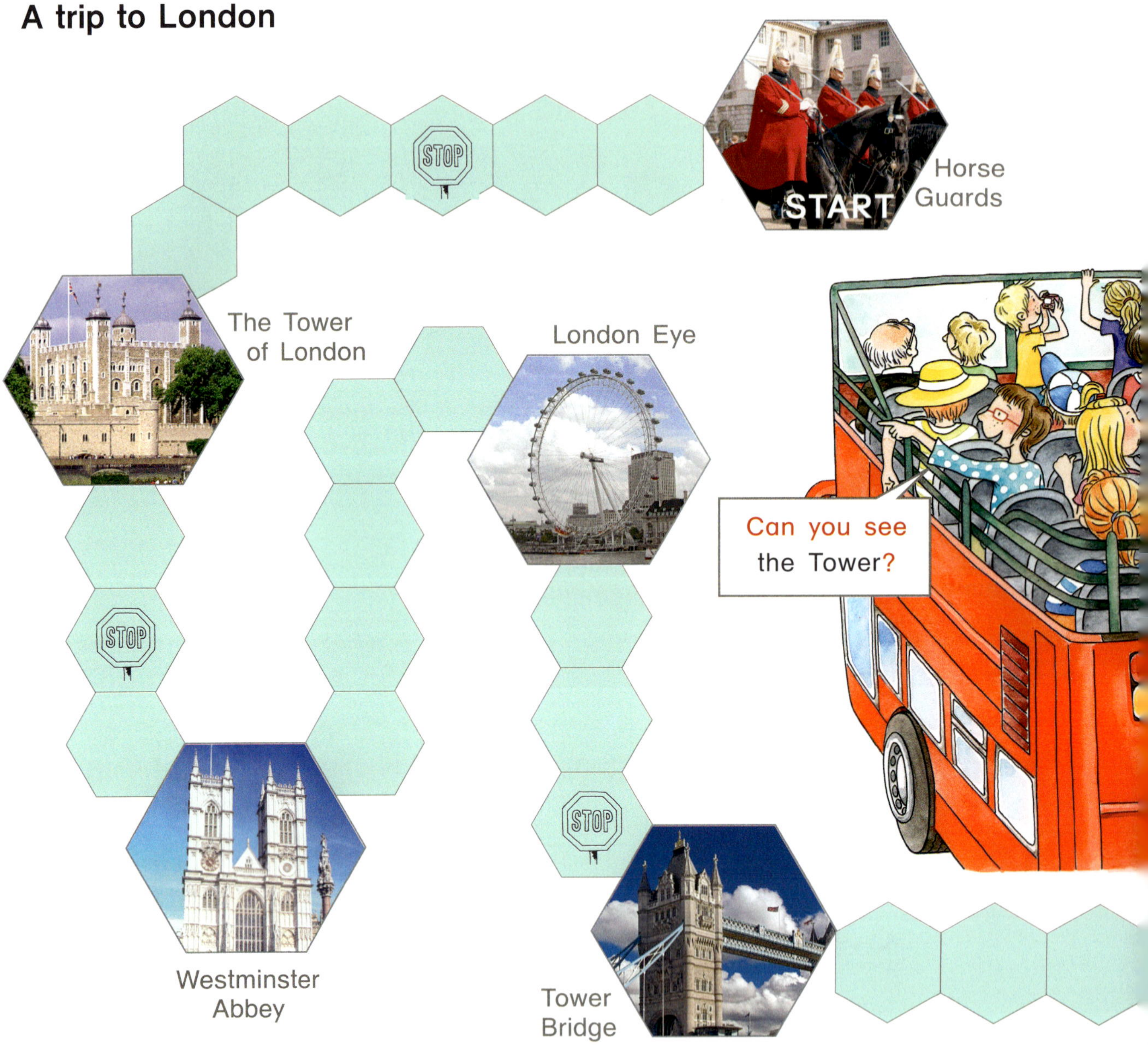

1 Listen and point to the pictures.

2 Listen to the sounds of London.

3 Play the game.

4 Find more information about London sights.

Roll the dice.
Move your counter.
STOP Miss a turn.

Londoner Sehenswürdigkeiten kennenlernen.
Diff ▾ KV 71

- FC/WC 118–135
- CD 49–51, KV 67/68/71
- WB S. 25

▸ Ich kann ein Spiel zu Londoner Sehenswürdigkeiten spielen.

What are the children doing?
How many people are on the bus?
How can you get around in London?

What would you like to see in London?
Which sights are there in your home town?

▸ Ich kann etwas über den Hyde Park erzählen.

A day in Hyde Park

Hallo Leute,

heute war schönes Wetter und wir haben wie viele Londoner den Sonntag im Hyde Park verbracht. Papa, Martin und ich haben wie immer Fußball gespielt und Oma hat einen Liegestuhl *(deckchair)* gemietet und sich gesonnt. Nach einem tollen Picknick wollte Martin noch zum großen See, *the Serpentine*, und ein Tretboot mieten. Das war super! Weil wir so müde waren, sind wir dann mit der U-Bahn, der *tube*, heimgefahren. Mit der *tube* ist man meistens am schnellsten in London unterwegs, selbst Taxis *(taxis/cabs)* brauchen länger.

Die Londoner U-Bahn ist übrigens die älteste U-Bahn der Welt. Sie wurde 1863 eröffnet. Auf den Rolltreppen, den *escalators*, die zu den U-Bahnen hinunterführen, sollte man eine wichtige Regel beachten: *Stand on the right!* Denn nur so können Fahrgäste, die es eilig haben, gut an den anderen vorbei kommen. Wer sich nicht an diese Regel hält, macht sich bei den Londonern sehr unbeliebt. Und auch ganz wichtig: *Mind the gap!* Habt ihr eine Idee, was das bedeuten könnte?

Ratet doch mal!

Eure müde

Lisa

1 Sprecht über Lisas Brief.

Informationen über den Hyde Park und öffentliche Verkehrsmittel in London erhalten.
Den Song *Mind the gap* (CD 57/58, KV 69) singen.

- CD (57/58)
- KV 69

▸ Ich kann sagen, wo ich in London hin will und wie ich da hinkomme.

Let's talk: Sightseeing in London

	Where?	How?	What?
⚀	London Eye	on the underground	buy a souvenir
⚁	Tower Bridge	by taxi	go for a walk
⚂	The Tower of London	by double-decker bus	visit
⚃	Big Ben	by bike	take photos
⚄	Hyde Park	by car	listen to a band
⚅	Buckingham Palace	on foot	have a snack

1 Listen and point.

2 Practise the dialogue.

3 Play the game.

At Hyde Park Café

1 Listen and point.

2 Read the menu. What would you like to have?

3 Write: I'd like to have ...

Look up more words in a dictionary.

Einen Bestelldialog in einem Café verstehen.
Eigene Dialoge ausdenken und führen.
Wdh: Food, drinks, money

• CD 53
• KV 72–75

▸ Ich kann englische Informationen ins Deutsche übertragen.

A day in Windsor Castle

1 Listen. What is the text about?

2 Read the information on the notice board. Explain it in German.

3 Practise the dialogues.

Children of the world

1 Listen and read along.

2 Listen and find out more about the children.

3 Find more English speaking countries.

Sich auf einer Weltkarte orientieren.
Den Song *We are here together* (CD 63/64, KV 88) singen.
Diff ▲ KV 80, Diff ▼ 79, Wdh: Bekannte Strukturen

- CD 60, (63/64)
- KV 78–81/88

▸ Ich kann verstehen, was die Kinder über sich erzählen.

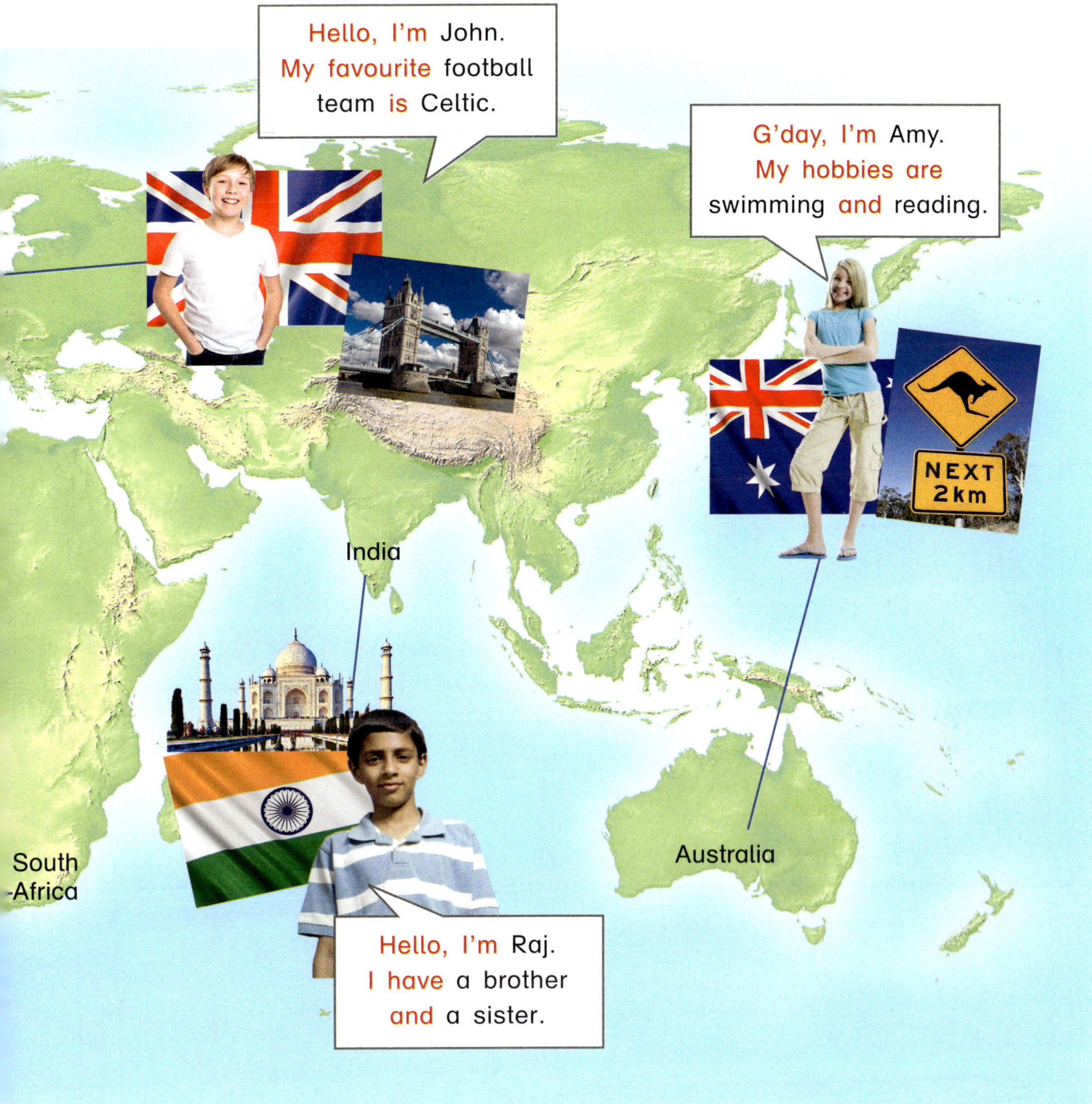

Can you ask questions to the answers?
Can you answer these questions?

Do you know other countries?
Do you have friends in other countries?

Lisa's letter: Curry, the new national dish

Hi ihr in Deutschland,

bei mir an der Schule findet diese Woche eine *international food campaign* statt. London ist eine echte Multikultistadt, in der Menschen aus rund 200 Nationen leben. Viele der *foreign born residents*, wie sie hier genannt werden, kommen zum Beispiel aus der Karibik, Afrika oder Indien.
Wir hatten die Aufgabe, ausländische Rezepte zu suchen, die dann in der Schulküche umgesetzt wurden. Meine Klasse hat sich für das neue „englische Nationalgericht" entschieden: ein indisches Curry.
Ravis Vater hat uns gezeigt, wie man das ganz original kocht.
Yummy, das war lecker! Ich bin gespannt, was es morgen gibt. Bis bald!

Eure Lisa

1 Lest Lisas Brief. Sprecht darüber.

2 Find out more about British food. 

▸ Ich kann etwas über die *flying doctors* erzählen.

A letter from Amy

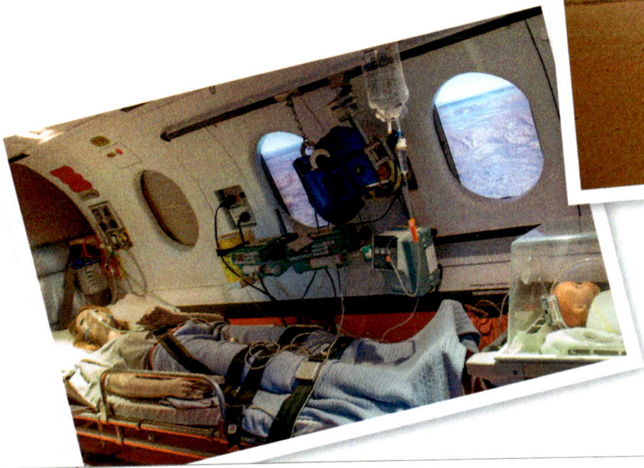

Hello everybody,

I am Amy from Adelaide / Australia.
My hobbies are swimming and reading and I'm a member of a boomerang club.
When I grow up I want to be a flying doctor. Flying doctors are important because a lot of people live on farms in the outback, far away from cities and hospitals. So the doctor has to come to them when they are ill. To become a flying doctor you have to learn to fly a small plane. I think this is a fascinating job.
I'm also interested in other countries and cultures. Perhaps you would like to write back and tell me about your home country?

Amy

1 Read Amy's letter. Talk about it.

2 Find out more about the flying doctors.

A letter from Gemma

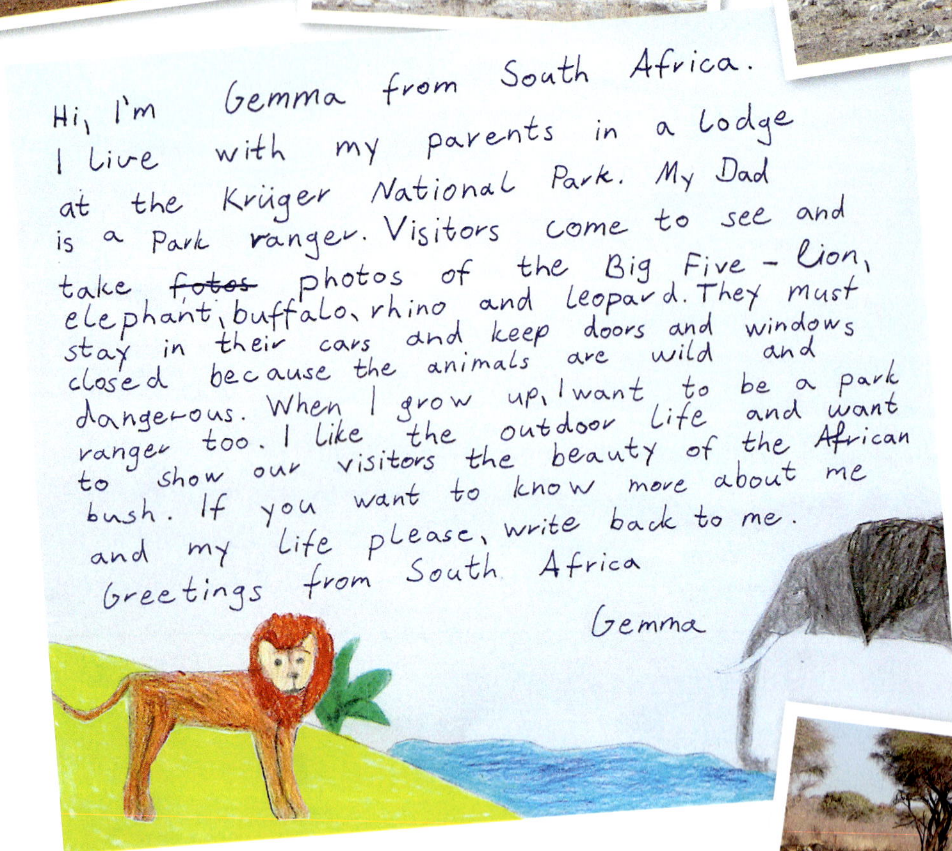

Hi, I'm Gemma from South Africa.
I live with my parents in a lodge
at the Krüger National Park. My Dad
is a park ranger. Visitors come to see and
take ~~fotos~~ photos of the Big Five – lion,
elephant, buffalo, rhino and leopard. They must
stay in their cars and keep doors and windows
closed because the animals are wild and
dangerous. When I grow up, I want to be a park
ranger too. I like the outdoor life and want
to show our visitors the beauty of the African
bush. If you want to know more about me
and my life please, write back to me.
Greetings from South Africa

Gemma

1 Read Gemma's letter. Talk about it.

2 Find out more about the Kruger National Park.

▸ Ich kann mein Lapbook präsentieren.

Let's talk: My lapbook

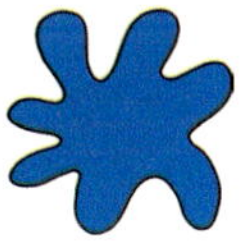

My favourite books are about horses.
My favourite subjects are maths and music.
I like dancing.

Tipp
I like ...ing.

1 Listen.

2 Listen again. Take notes.

3 Make your own lapbook. Present it.

Ein Lapbook erstellen und vorstellen.
Diff ▲ KV 87, Diff ▼ 86
Wdh: About me, friends, hobbies, favourite things ...

• CD 61
• KV 82–87

Jack and the beanstalk

 money  market  magic beans  cow

 giant  hen  golden eggs  axe

 man  castle  beanstalk

There is a boy named Jack.

He lives with his mother. They have no  .

One day Jack's mother says, **"We must sell our**  . Take it to the  ."

On his way to the  Jack meets a  .

The  **gives Jack 5** 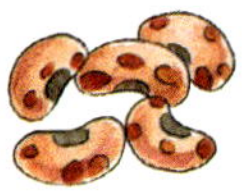 **for the**  .

Jack's mother is very angry.

She throws the 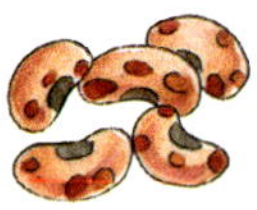 **out of the window.**

1 Listen to the story. What is it about?

2 Read the text out loud.

3 Tell the story in German.

4 Act it out.

Eine traditionelle Geschichte kennenlernen.
Einen Lesetext erarbeiten.
Diff ▲ L liest die Geschichte selbst.

• FC/WC 136–146
• CD 65

The next morning, **there is a big**  in front of the window.

Jack climbs up the  . He climbs up higher and higher.

When he is at the top, **Jack sees a beautiful**  **. He goes inside.**

There is a big  sleeping in the kitchen.

The  **has a**  **that can lay**  **.**

Jack takes the  **to take it home.**

Suddenly the  wakes up and runs after Jack.

Jack runs faster. He climbs down the  .

The  **runs after him.**

Jack shouts, "Mother, help, help!"

Jack's mother takes an  **and cuts down the**  **.**

The  falls to the ground.

Nobody ever sees the  **again**. And Jack and his mother?

They live happily ever after and the  **lays many**  **.**

Treasure Island

Jim finds a treasure map. He and his friends want to find the treasure.

They sail to Treasure Island with John Silver and his crew. One night, Jim finds out that they are pirates.

On the island Jim meets Ben Gunn. He knows where the treasure is.

John Silver and his pirates look for the treasure but can't find it.

There is a big fight.

Jim and his friends escape with the treasure and sail home. And John Silver?

1 Listen to the story.

2 Read it out loud.

3 Talk about your favourite stories.

Eine Bildergeschichte verstehen.
Diff ▾ L liest die Geschichte selbst.
Diff ▴ Die Geschichte mit KV 89/93 selbst lesen.

- SC 16–21
- CD 66
- KV 89/93

The treasure hunt

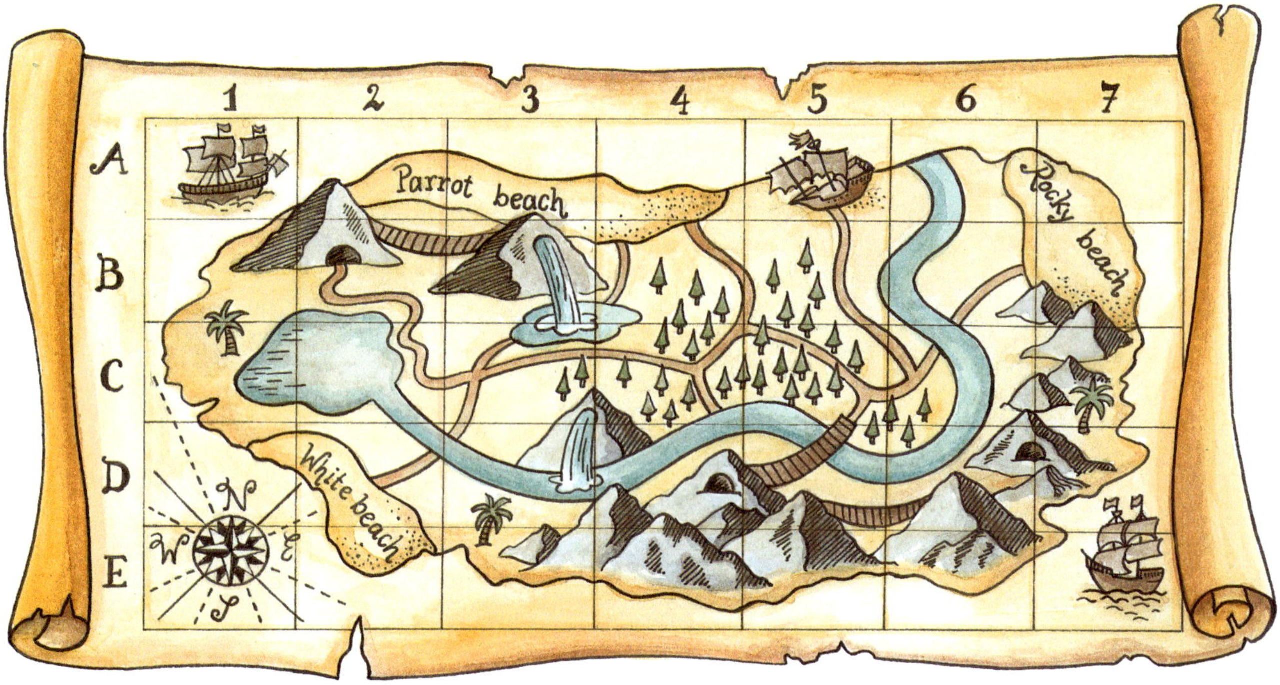

land at ... beach

walk through the forest

swim through the river

walk into the cave

dive under the waterfall

walk around the lake

climb the rock

walk over the rope bridge

1 Listen and find the treasure.

2 Hide a treasure. Tell your partner the way.

Eine Wegbeschreibung in natürlichem Gelände geben.
Wdh: Directions

- CD 67
- KV 90

▸ Ich kann etwas über Halloween in Großbritannien sagen.

Halloween in Great Britain

Hallo Leute!

Trick or treat! Wisst ihr, was das bedeutet? Ich habe gehört, dass ihr auch in Deutschland jetzt immer Halloween feiert. Hier ist in den letzten Tagen des Oktobers wirklich viel los. Viele Kinder basteln sich lustige Verkleidungen, aber manche kaufen sich auch richtige Kostüme, um möglichst gruselig auszusehen. Ich habe mich mit alten Kleidungsstücken von Mama als Hexe *(witch)* verkleidet und mich schwarz und weiß geschminkt. Am Abend des 31. Oktobers sind wir dann durch die Straßen gelaufen und haben an ganz vielen Haustüren geklingelt. Wenn die Tür geöffnet wurde, haben wir laut *Trick or treat!* gerufen und dafür jede Menge Süßigkeiten bekommen.
Was ruft ihr zu Halloween?
Schaurige Grüße von
eurer Lisa

Mein cooler *jack-o'-lantern*

1 Sprecht über Lisas Brief. Was macht ihr an Halloween?

Informationen über Halloween in Großbritannien erhalten.
Diff ▲ KV 91

• KV 91
• WB S. 32

▸ Ich kann etwas über den St. Patrick's Day erzählen.

St Patrick's Day

Hey ihr,

gestern war ich bei meinem Freund Aiden eingeladen. Seine Familie kommt aus Irland und wir feierten gemeinsam Sankt Patrick's Day.
Sankt Patrick war ein Heiliger (so ein wenig wie Sankt Martin) und lebte vor über 1500 Jahre in Irland. Er erzählte den Menschen von Gott und gab ihnen hilfreiche Ratschläge. Jedes Jahr am 17. März erinnern Iren überall auf der Welt an den Heiligen Sankt Patrick.
Sie ziehen sich grün an, tragen große grüne Hüte und schmücken alles mit Kleeblättern (das war das Erkennungszeichen von Sankt Patrick).
Bei Aiden gab es dann auch nur Grünes zu essen und zu trinken und wir haben im Fernsehen eine Sankt-Patrick's-Parade aus Chikago angeschaut. Da war richtig was los. Es spielten Musikgruppen, es wurde getanzt und alle sahen sehr fröhlich aus. Stellt euch vor, sie haben sogar den Fluss *(river)* mit Lebensmittelfarbe grün gefärbt.

Slán (das heißt Tschüß auf Irisch),
Lisa

1 Lest Lisas Brief.

2 Kennt ihr ähnliche Bräuche?

The story of the leprechaun

One day a young man walked through a forest in Ireland.
Suddenly he heard the tap-tapping of a small hammer.

It came from a leprechaun who was repairing a shoe.

The man knew that leprechauns have a pot of gold. So he grabbed the leprechaun and asked, "Where is your pot of gold?"

1 Listen to the story.

2 Read the story.

3 Do a role-play.

Eine mythologische Figur kennenlernen.
Den Song *Leprechaun* (CD 69/70) singen.

- SC 22–29
- CD 68–70

▸ Ich kann eine Geschichte verstehen.

The leprechaun said,
"The pot of gold … eh … is … eh …
over there, under the bush."

The man marked the bush
with his red scarf.

"Don't take my scarf away!",
he said to the leprechaun.

The man ran home to get a spade.
The leprechaun was left behind.

When the man came back with his spade, the leprechaun was gone.
But there was a red scarf on every bush in the forest.
Poor man – the leprechaun had played a trick on him.

Fit for 5: Superbrain

	People	Places	Activities
1	Who is John Silver? 100	Where does Ben live? 100	What does Jim want to do on Treasure Island? 100
2	Who is Robo? 80	Where is Hyde Park? 80	What do you do at 7 o'clock in the morning? 80
3	Who is Jack? 60	Where do kangaroos live? 60	What does Emma's mum do on Friday? 60
4	Who is playing football on Friday? 40	Where can you watch the feeding of the seals? 40	What has Ben got to do before Lisa visits him? 40
5	Who is Ray? 20	Where is Hyde Park Café? 20	What do you do in ICT? 20
6	Who are Lisa's best friends? 10	Where is Samuel from? 10	What do you do at school? 10
	People	Places	Activities

1 Answer the questions.

2 Think of more questions.

People	Places	Activities	
Who was St Patrick? 100	Where do people colour a river green? 100	What does Gemma want to do when she grows up? 100	1
Who is asking the way to Baker Street? 80	Where do you brush your teeth? 80	What happens on St Patrick's Day? 80	2
Who runs after Jack? 60	Where do parrots originally live? 60	What can you eat at Hyde Park Café? 60	3
Who does Jim meet on the island? 40	Where do you cook? 40	What can you do in London? 40	4
Who lives in Canada and likes skiing? 20	Where do llamas live? 20	What can you do during golden time? 20	5
Who is from New York? 10	Where does Amy live? 10	What can you do after school? 10	6
People	Places	Activities	

How to learn words

Ich höre mir das Wort auf der CD an und spreche es nach.

Ich schreibe die Wörter auf Merkzettel und verteile sie im Raum.

Ich verwende das Wort in einem Satz.

Das hilft mir beim Lernen von Wörtern.

Ich beschrifte Bilder.

Ich sage mir das Wort immer wieder laut vor.

Ich arbeite mit einem Vokabelkasten.

Ich mache eine passende Bewegung und sage das Wort.

Ich spiele mit meinen Kärtchen ein Wörterspiel wie Memo oder Domino.

How to communicate

Ich spreche meine Gesprächspartner direkt an und schaue sie dabei an.

Ich versuche in ganzen Sätzen zu sprechen.

Wenn mich meine Gesprächspartner nicht verstehen, wiederhole ich meine Sätze langsam und deutlich. Ich kann meine Sätze durch deutliche Gesichtsausdrücke und Gesten unterstützen.

Das hilft mir beim Sprechen.

Wenn ich etwas nicht verstehe, sage ich: „Sorry, I don't understand“. Wenn meine Gesprächspartner einen Satz nicht formulieren können, versuche ich ihnen zu helfen.

Wenn nötig, zeige ich auf Gegenstände oder Personen.

Wenn ich etwas beim ersten Mal nicht verstehe, sage ich: „Can you say it again, please?“

Durch meine Betonung im Satz kann ich deutlich machen, dass ich etwas frage.

How to do a presentation

Das hilft mir beim Erstellen einer Präsentation.

Ich schlage Wörter zu einem Thema in einem Wörterbuch nach und sammle sie.

Ich ordne Stichwörter in einer Mindmap.

Ich überlege mir passende Sätze.

Ich suche Bilder aus und schreibe Stichwörter dazu auf.

Ich fertige ein Poster an.

Ich übe meinen Vortrag.

Wenn ich nicht weiß, wie ich ein Wort ausspreche, frage ich andere Kinder oder meine Lehrkraft.

Wenn mir ein Wort während der Präsentation nicht einfällt, stelle ich es pantomimisch dar oder zeige darauf, wenn es in meiner Nähe ist.

Beim Vortragen schaue ich meine Zuhörenden an und versuche frei und deutlich zu sprechen.

How to do a role-play

Beim Spielen sprechen wir laut und deutlich.

Wir hören uns Musterdialoge auf der CD an.

Wir spielen anderen Kindern vor und fragen nach ihrer Meinung.

Das hilft mir beim Vorbereiten eines Rollenspiels.

Wenn wir nicht wissen, wie man ein Wort ausspricht, fragen wir unsere Lehrkraft.

Wir überlegen, was wir sagen wollen.

Wir üben die Wörter und Sätze.

Wir schauen auf den *Let's talk*-Seiten nach, was wir sagen könnten.

Wir verteilen die Rollen.

A

act out	vorspielen, aufführen
activity	die Tätigkeit
adult	der/die Erwachsene
after	nach
again	wieder
all	alle, alles
along	entlang
animal	das Tier
anorak	der Anorak
antelope	die Antilope
ape	der Menschenaffe
art	der Kunstunterricht
axe	die Axt

B

balcony	der Balkon
bamboo	der Bambus
bathroom	das Badezimmer
beach	der Strand
beak	der Schnabel
beanstalk	die Bohnenranke
bear	der Bär
beautiful	wunderschön
because	weil
bed	das Bett
bedroom	das Schlafzimmer
behind	hinter
between	zwischen
bin	der Mülleimer
bite	beißen
blackboard	die Tafel
board game	das Brettspiel
boat	das Boot
body part	das Körperteil
bookshelf	das Bücherregal
boomerang	der Boomerang
boots	die Stiefel
bottle	die Flasche
break	die Pause
bridge	die Brücke
British	britisch
brush my hair	meine Haare bürsten
brush my teeth	meine Zähne putzen
buffalo	der Büffel
build	bauen
bunk bed	das Stockbett
buried	vergraben
bush	der Busch
buy	kaufen
bye	Tschüss

C

camel	das Kamel
car	das Auto
carpet	der Teppich
castle	das Schloss
catch	fangen
cave	die Höhle
celebrate	feiern
cellar	der Keller
chicken	das Huhn, das Hähnchen
chimpanzee	der Schimpanse
church	die Kirche
cinema	das Kino
circle	der Kreis, einkreisen
climb	klettern
cloud	die Wolke
cloudy	bewölkt
coat	der Mantel
collect stickers	Aufkleber sammeln
colour	die Farbe, anmalen
command	die Anweisung
compare	vergleichen
complete	vervollständigen
copy	die Kopie, kopieren
count	zählen
country	das Land
crafts	der Werkunterricht
crew	die Mannschaft
crocodile	das Krokodil
cupboard	der Schrank

D

dangerous	gefährlich
deckchair	der Liegestuhl
describe	beschreiben
desk	der Schreibtisch
destroy	zerstören
dice	der Würfel
dictionary	das Wörterbuch
dig	graben
dinner	das warme Essen
disabled	behindert, beeinträchtigt
dive	tauchen
door	die Tür
double-decker bus	der Doppeldeckerbus

down	hinunter
draw	zeichnen
dress	das Kleid, anziehen
drink	das Getränk, trinken

E

elephant	der Elefant
endangered	gefährdet
enemy	der Feind
English	Englisch
entry	der Eintritt
escalator	die Rolltreppe
escape	entkommen, flüchten
everybody	jeder, jede
explain	erklären

F

far	weit
feather	die Feder
feed	füttern
feeling	das Gefühl
female	weiblich
Ferris wheel	das Riesenrad
fight	der Kampf
find (out)	(heraus-)finden
fireplace	der offene Kamin
first	der/die/das Erste
fish	der Fisch
flag	die Flagge
flat	die Wohnung
flipper	die Flosse
fly	fliegen
foggy	nebelig
food	das Essen
forest	der Wald
free entry	der freie Eintritt
free time	die Freizeit
fun	der Spaß, lustig
furniture	die Möbel
future	die Zukunft

G

game	das Spiel
garden	der Garten
German	deutsch
get dressed	anziehen
get up	aufstehen
giant	der Riese
give	geben
gloves	die Fingerhandschuhe
glue	der Klebstoff, kleben
go to bed	zu Bett gehen
go to school	zur Schule gehen
golden time	der Freiarbeitsunterricht
goodbye	auf Wiedersehen
grab	fassen, packen
grassland	die Graslandschaft
great	toll, super
grow up	aufwachsen

H

habitat	der Lebensraum
hair	das Haar, die Haare
hamster	der Hamster
hand	die Hand
have breakfast	frühstücken
have dinner	warm essen
have lunch	(zu) Mittag essen
head	der Kopf
hear	hören
heart	das Herz
help	die Hilfe, helfen
hen	die Henne
here	hier
high	hoch
holiday	der Feiertag, der Urlaub
homework	die Hausaufgaben
hoof, hooves	der Huf, die Hufe
horn	das Horn
horse	das Pferd
hospital	das Krankenhaus
hot	heiß
house	das Haus
how	wie
hunt	jagen

I

ice cream	die Eiscreme
ICT	der Computerunterricht
in front of	vor
in	in
insect	das Insekt
instruction	die Anleitung
intelligent	intelligent
island	die Insel

J

joy . . . . die Freude
juice . . . . der Saft
jump . . . . springen

K

kangaroo . . . . . . das Känguru
keyword . . . . das Schlüsselwort
kick . . . . treten
kitchen . . . . die Küche

L

label . . . . beschriften
lake . . . . der See
lamp . . . . die Lampe
language . . . . . . die Sprache
lay . . . . legen
left . . . . links, übrig
leopard . . . . der Leopard
library . . . . die Bücherei
life span . . . . . . die Lebenserwartung
line . . . . die Zeile, die Strophe
lion . . . . der Löwe
list . . . . die Liste, auflisten
little . . . . klein
live . . . . leben
living room . . . . . das Wohnzimmer
lose . . . . verlieren

M

magic . . . . die Magie, magisch
make . . . . machen, tun
male . . . . männlich
man . . . . der Mann
mane . . . . die Mähne
market . . . . der Markt
maths . . . . der Mathematikunterricht
meat . . . . das Fleisch
mend . . . . reparieren
menu . . . . die Speisekarte
mighty . . . . mächtig
monkey . . . . der Affe
mountain . . . . . . der Berg
mouse . . . . die Maus
move . . . . bewegen
much . . . . viel
music . . . . der Musikunterricht

N

neck . . . . der Hals
neckerchief . . . . . das Halstuch
next to . . . . neben
nobody . . . . niemand
noisy . . . . laut
nothing . . . . nichts
nut . . . . die Nuss

O

oil . . . . das Öl
old . . . . alt
on . . . . auf, im
on foot . . . . zu Fuß
other . . . . andere, anderer, anderes
out . . . . raus
outback . . . . abgelegenes Gebiet Australiens
own . . . . eigene, eigener, eigenes

P

pair . . . . das Paar, Paare bilden
palace . . . . der Palast
panda . . . . der Pandabär
parrot . . . . der Papagei
part . . . . das Teil
path . . . . der Pfad
paw . . . . die Pfote
PE . . . . der Sportunterricht
penguin . . . . der Pinguin
phone . . . . das Telefon, telefonieren
pick up . . . . aufheben
pirate . . . . der Pirat
plan . . . . planen
plant . . . . die Pflanze
pocket . . . . die (Hosen-)Tasche
polar bear . . . . . der Eisbär
pouch . . . . Beutel, Tasche
promise . . . . versprechen
protect . . . . schützen
pullover . . . . der Pullover
put . . . . legen

R

rabbit . . . . der Hase, das Kaninchen

raincoat	der Regenmantel
rainy	regnerisch
read	lesen
recorder	die Blockflöte
remember	erinnern
rhino	das Nashorn
ride	fahren, reiten
right	rechts, richtig
river	der Fluss
roar	brüllen
rock	der Felsen
room	das Zimmer
rope bridge	die Seilbrücke
run	rennen, laufen

S

sail	segeln
scared	ängstlich
scarf	der Schal
science	der Sachunterricht
seal	der Seehund
share	teilen
ship	das Schiff
shirt	das Hemd
shoes	die Schuhe
show	zeigen
shy	schüchtern, scheu
sights	die Sehenswürdigkeiten
skirt	der Rock
skyscraper	der Wolkenkratzer
sleep	schlafen
snake	die Schlange
snowy	verschneit
socks	die Socken
sofa	das Sofa
souvenir	das Andenken
spade	der Spaten
special	besonders
spin	drehen
spit	spucken
stairs	die Treppe
stormy	stürmisch
straight ahead	geradeaus
strong	stark
subject	das Unterrichtsfach
suddenly	plötzlich
sunny	sonnig

T

tail	der Schwanz
take (out)	(heraus-)nehmen
task	die Aufgabe
tell	erzählen, sagen
then	dann
there	da
through	durch
tidy up	aufräumen
tiger	der Tiger
timetable	der Stundenplan
tiny	winzig
tonight	heute Abend/Nacht
tooth, teeth	der Zahn, die Zähne
treasure	der Schatz
tree nest	das Baumnest
trousers	die Hose
trunk	hier: der Rüssel
turn	umdrehen, abbiegen

U

underground	die Untergrundbahn
up	hinauf
use	benutzen

W

wallet	der Geldbeutel
wardrobe	der Kleiderschrank
watch (TV)	(fern-)sehen
waterfall	der Wasserfall
way	der Weg
wear	tragen
where	wo
who	wer
windy	windig
wish	der Wunsch, wünschen
woolly hat	die (Woll)Mütze
world	die Welt
write (down)	(auf-)schreiben

Z

zebra	das Zebra
zoo	der Zoo
zookeeper	der Tierpfleger, die Tierpflegerin

Bildquellennachweis

|Alamy Stock Photo (RMB), Abingdon/Oxfordshire: Angela Hampton Picture Library 50.1; Elizabeth Whiting & Associates 24.1; Holmes Garden Photos 34.3; Hopkins, Cindy 43.2; Hornak, Angelo 34.1; Jordan, Peter 31.3; Juniors Bildarchiv 30.3; Kord, Russell 34.6; Kuttig 35.4; Mega, Marco 31.4; schrama, ilse 43.1, 43.5; Turner, Bob 35.1. |Assies, Juliane, Berlin: 3.30, 17.1, 17.4, 17.5, 17.6, 17.8, 17.9, 17.10, 17.11, 17.12, 17.13, 17.14, 20.5, 27.1, 27.2, 27.3, 27.4, 27.5, 27.6, 27.7, 45.2, 45.3. |fotolia.com, New York: clickit 30.16; Divizia, Claudio 24.3; Hackemann, Jörg 41.8; immrchris 24.2; Jukna, Aigars 36.3; Kosmider, Patryk 40.3; Licht und Blindheit 35.9, 36.1; lucamedei 40.7; Monkey Business 50.5; OHRAUGE 34.8, 41.5; rcfotostock 40.5; Shepulova, Anna 42.2; somartin 40.4; Spencer 41.1; vichie81 35.11. |Garbert, Jutta, Nürnberg: 12.4, 12.6, 18.2, 18.3, 24.4, 30.2, 30.6, 30.7, 30.8, 30.9, 30.10, 30.11, 30.12, 30.14, 30.15, 33.3, 33.4, 33.5, 33.6, 35.15, 37.13, 42.3, 50.3, 51.5, 51.7. |Getty Images (RF), München: Bobbe, Leland 41.9; Radius Images 40.2; Rubberball/Kemp, Mike 41.4, 43.4. |Glökler, Angela (Atelier echtgelb), Hamburg: Titel, Titel. |Hilgert, Gabie, Hamburg: 7.41, 20.1, 29.10. |Holzhausen, Elisabeth, Wedel: 57.3, 57.4, 58.1, 58.6, 58.7, 58.10, 59.1, 59.2, 59.3, 59.7, 59.8, 59.9. |iStockphoto.com, Calgary: Titel; aabejon 40.12, 44.6; Baggett, Anthony 40.9; Davoust, Laurent 41.3; Heger, Jonathan 40.10; Locke, Sean 40.8; Moller, Karen 41.6; visual7 40.1, 40.11, 41.7, 41.10. |juniors@wildlife Bildagentur GmbH, Hamburg: Zoellner, B. 30.5. |Kehr, Karoline, Hamburg: 35.16, 37.8, 37.11. |Manz, Stephanie, Berlin: 37.2, 37.4, 37.6, 37.9, 37.10, 37.12. |mauritius images GmbH, Mittenwald: Frei, Nora 42.5; Loop Images 42.1; Lumi Images/Pupeter-Secen 40.6; World Pictures 43.3. |Muth, Matthias, Biederitz: 34.4. |PantherMedia GmbH (panthermedia.net), München: Sztanek, Thomas 24.6. |Picture-Alliance GmbH, Frankfurt/M.: dpa 30.13; NHPA/photoshot 30.1. |primanota GmbH, Korbach: 31.1. |Ruthe, Oda, Braunschweig: 5.32, 5.34, 5.37, 5.38, 5.39, 5.40, 5.41, 5.42, 6.29, 6.38, 7.31, 9.29, 10.30, 10.31, 10.34, 11.10, 11.11, 11.12, 11.13, 11.14, 11.15, 11.16, 11.17, 12.5, 15.1, 16.1, 18.1, 22.3, 23.2, 23.5, 23.6, 23.7, 23.9, 23.10, 24.5, 31.2, 33.2, 34.2, 34.5, 34.7, 34.13, 34.14, 34.17, 35.8, 35.13, 36.4, 38.1, 39.1, 39.2, 42.4, 45.6, 48.2, 48.3, 48.4, 48.5, 48.6, 48.7, 49.2, 49.3, 49.4, 49.5, 49.6, 49.7, 49.8, 49.9, 49.10, 50.2, 50.4, 51.6, 52.1, 53.1, 53.2. |Schönau, Michaela, Stuttgart: 44.2, 44.3, 44.4, 44.7. |Schumann, Friederike, Berlin: 1.13, 1.13, 1.26, 1.27, 1.28, 2.13, 2.26, 2.27, 2.28, 2.29, 2.30, 2.32, 2.35, 2.36, 2.37, 2.39, 3.13, 3.13, 3.13, 3.13, 3.13, 3.13, 3.13, 3.13, 3.13, 3.13, 3.13, 3.27, 4.13, 4.26, 4.27, 4.28, 4.29, 5.1, 5.14, 5.14, 5.14, 5.14, 5.14, 5.14, 5.14, 5.14, 5.14, 5.14, 5.14, 5.14, 5.14, 5.27, 5.27, 5.27, 5.27, 5.27, 5.27, 5.27, 5.27, 5.27, 5.27, 5.27, 5.27, 5.27, 5.28, 5.29, 5.30, 5.31, 5.33, 5.35, 5.36, 6.1, 6.14, 6.27, 6.28, 6.30, 6.31, 6.32, 6.33, 6.34, 7.13, 7.13, 7.13, 7.13, 7.13, 7.13, 7.13, 7.13, 7.13, 7.13, 7.13, 7.13, 7.14, 7.15, 7.28, 7.29, 7.30, 7.32, 7.33, 7.34, 7.35, 7.36, 7.37, 7.38, 7.39, 7.40, 8.14, 8.14, 8.14, 8.14, 8.14, 8.14, 8.14, 8.14, 8.14, 8.14, 8.14, 8.14, 8.28, 8.28, 8.28, 8.28, 8.28, 8.28, 8.28, 8.28, 8.28, 8.28, 8.28, 8.28, 8.28, 8.28, 8.30, 9.13, 9.13, 9.13, 9.13, 9.13, 9.13, 9.13, 9.13, 9.13, 9.13, 9.26, 10.14, 10.14, 10.14, 10.14, 10.14, 10.14, 10.14, 10.14, 10.14, 10.14, 10.14, 10.14, 10.14, 10.14, 10.28, 10.28, 10.28, 10.28, 10.28, 10.28, 10.28, 10.28, 10.28, 10.28, 10.28, 10.28, 10.28, 10.28, 10.29, 11.1, 11.2, 11.3, 11.4, 11.5, 11.6, 11.7, 11.8, 11.9, 13.2, 14.1, 17.2, 17.3, 17.7, 19.1, 20.2, 20.3, 20.4, 20.6, 20.7, 20.8, 20.9, 22.1, 22.2, 23.1, 23.3, 23.4, 23.8, 23.11, 23.12, 23.13, 23.14, 23.15, 25.2, 25.7, 26.1, 26.2, 26.3, 26.4, 26.5, 27.8, 27.9, 28.1, 28.2, 28.3, 28.4, 29.1, 29.2, 29.3, 29.4, 29.5, 29.6, 29.7, 29.8, 29.9, 29.11, 29.12, 29.13, 29.14, 29.15, 29.16, 30.4, 33.9, 34.9, 35.2, 35.3, 35.5, 35.6, 35.7, 35.10, 35.12, 35.14, 37.3, 37.5, 37.7, 38.2, 44.1, 45.4, 45.7, 45.8, 46.2, 46.3, 46.4, 46.5, 46.6, 46.7, 46.8, 46.9, 46.10, 46.11, 46.12, 46.13, 46.14, 46.15, 46.16, 46.17, 46.18, 46.19, 46.20, 46.21, 46.22, 47.2, 47.3, 47.4, 47.5, 47.6, 47.7, 47.8, 47.9, 47.10, 47.11, 47.12, 47.13, 47.14, 47.15, 47.16, 47.17, 47.18, 47.19, 50.6. |Shutterstock.com, New York: astudio 51.2; Baranov, E 12.1; dade72 36.5; de Marmore, Cabeca 18.5; GUDKOV, ANDREY 32.3; Holm, Stefan 12.8; Jenner, Chris 36.2; Maxisport 12.7; Monk, Stuart 51.3, 51.4; Monkey Business Images 6.39; Shashkina, Elena 51.8; stuar 18.4; Sunghee, Kang 3.33; The Road Provides 32.1; Thitipat, Nook 12.3; Uryadnikov, Sergey 32.2; Vasilis, Ververidis 12.2; vichie81 51.1. |stock.adobe.com, Dublin: pololia 3.31, 41.2. |Tauber, Andreas, Berlin: 3.32, 3.34, 3.35, 7.42, 8.29, 8.31, 8.32, 13.1, 13.3, 13.4, 13.5, 13.6, 21.1, 21.2, 21.3, 21.4, 25.1, 25.3, 25.4, 25.5, 25.6, 33.1, 33.7, 33.8, 37.1, 37.14, 45.1, 45.5. |Van Montagu, Anna, Ahaus: 44.5. |Vetter, Ulrike, Leipzig: 3.36, 3.37, 3.38, 3.39, 3.40, 4.30, 4.31, 4.32, 4.33, 6.35, 6.36, 6.37, 7.43, 7.44, 7.45, 7.46, 8.33, 8.34, 8.35, 8.37, 9.30, 9.31, 9.32, 9.33, 9.34, 9.35, 10.32, 10.33, 10.35, 13.7, 13.8, 13.9, 14.2, 14.3, 14.4, 15.2, 15.3, 15.4, 16.2, 16.3, 16.4, 19.2, 19.3, 19.4, 19.5, 19.6, 20.10, 20.11, 21.5, 21.6, 21.8, 22.4, 22.5, 22.6, 22.7, 25.8, 25.9, 25.10, 26.6, 26.7, 26.8, 27.10, 27.11, 27.12, 27.13, 27.14, 28.5, 28.6, 28.7, 28.8, 30.17, 30.18, 30.19, 31.5, 31.6, 32.4, 32.5, 32.6, 33.10, 33.11, 33.12, 33.13, 33.14, 34.10, 34.11, 34.12, 34.15, 37.15, 37.16, 37.17, 37.19, 38.3, 38.4, 38.5, 38.6, 38.7, 39.3, 39.4, 39.5, 39.6, 39.7, 40.13, 40.14, 40.15, 43.6, 44.8, 45.9, 45.10, 45.11, 46.23, 46.24, 46.25, 46.26, 46.27, 48.8, 48.9, 48.10, 48.11, 49.11, 49.12, 49.13, 52.2, 52.3, 52.4, 54.1, 54.2.

Wir arbeiten sehr sorgfältig daran, für alle verwendeten Abbildungen die Rechteinhaberinnen und Rechteinhaber zu ermitteln. Sollte uns dies im Einzelfall nicht vollständig gelungen sein, werden berechtigte Ansprüche selbstverständlich im Rahmen der üblichen Vereinbarungen abgegolten.